Hot Math Topics

Problem Solving, Communication, and Reasoning

Finding Patterns and Reasoning

grade
1

Carole Greenes
Linda Schulman Dacey
Rika Spungin

Dale Seymour Publications®
An imprint of Pearson Learning
Parsippany, New Jersey

Dale Seymour Publications
An imprint of Pearson Learning
299 Jefferson Road
Parsippany, NJ 07054-0480
www.pearsonlearning.com
1-800-321-3106

Editorial Manager: Carolyn Coyle
Project Editor: Mali Apple
Production/Manufacturing Director: Janet Yearian
Production/Manufacturing Manager: Karen Edmonds
Production/Manufacturing Coordinator: Lorraine Allen
Design Director: Phyllis Aycock
Text and Cover Design: Tracey Munz
Cover and Interior Illustrations: Jared Lee
Computer Graphics: Alan Noyes

Order number 27502
ISBN 0-7690-0832-1

1 2 3 4 5 6 7 8 9 10-ML-04 03 02 01 00

This Book Is Printed
On Recycled Paper

Contents

Introduction

Why Was *Hot Math Topics* Developed?

The *Hot Math Topics* series was developed for several reasons:

- to offer children practice and maintenance of previously learned skills and concepts
- to enhance problem solving and mathematical reasoning abilities
- to build literacy skills
- to nurture collaborative learning behaviors

Practicing and maintaining concepts and skills

Although textbooks and core curriculum materials do treat the topics explored in this series, their treatment is often limited by the lesson format and the page size. As a consequence, there are often not enough opportunities for children to practice newly acquired concepts and skills related to the topics, or to connect the topics to other content areas. *Hot Math Topics* provides the necessary practice and mathematical connections.

Similarly, core instructional programs often do not do a very good job of helping children maintain their skills. Although textbooks do include reviews of previously learned material, they are often limited to sidebars or boxed-off areas on one or two pages in each chapter, with four or five exercises in each box. Each set of problems is intended only as a sampling of previously taught topics, rather than as a complete review. In the selection and placement of the review exercises, little or no attention is given to levels of complexity of the problems. By contrast, *Hot Math Topics* targets specific topics and gives children more experience with concepts and skills related to them. The problems are sequenced by difficulty, allowing children to hone their skills. And, because they are not tied to specific lessons, the problems can be used at any time.

Enhancing problem solving and mathematical reasoning abilities

Hot Math Topics present children with situations in which they may use a variety of problem solving strategies, including

- designing and conducting experiments to generate or collect data
- guessing, checking, and revising guesses
- organizing data in lists or tables in order to identify patterns and relationships
- choosing appropriate computational algorithms and deciding on a sequence of computations
- using inverse operations in "work backward" solution paths

For their solutions, children are also required to bring to bear various methods of reasoning, including

- deductive reasoning
- inductive reasoning
- proportional reasoning

For example, to solve clue-type problems, children must reason deductively and make inferences about mathematical relationships in order to generate candidates for the solutions and to home in on those that meet all of the problem's conditions.

To identify and continue a pattern and then verbalize a rule for finding the next term in that pattern, children must reason inductively.

To find equivalent quantities and make trades, children must reason proportionally.

To estimate or compare magnitudes of numbers, or to determine the type of number appropriate for a given situation, children must apply their number sense skills.

Building communication and literacy skills

Hot Math Topics offers children opportunities to write and talk about mathematical ideas. For many problems, children must describe their solution paths, justify their solutions, give their opinions, or write or tell stories.

Some problems have multiple solution methods. With these problems, children may have to compare their methods with those of their peers and talk about how their approaches are alike and different.

Other problems have multiple solutions, requiring children to confer to be sure they have found all possible answers.

Nurturing collaborative learning behaviors

Several of the problems can be solved by children working together. Some are designed specifically as partner problems. By working collaboratively, children can develop expertise in posing questions that call for clarification or verification, brainstorming solution strategies, and following another person's line of reasoning.

What Is in *Finding Patterns and Reasoning*?

This book contains 100 problems and tasks that focus on reasoning and finding patterns. The mathematics content, the mathematical connections, the problem solving strategies, and the communication skills that are emphasized are described below.

Mathematics content

Problems and tasks involving patterns and reasoning require children to

- identify, complete, extend, and create repeating and growing patterns
- interpret comparative language to solve problems
- use deductive, inductive, proportional, spatial, and algebraic reasoning to solve problems
- identify and describe similarities and differences among elements in a set and between sets

Mathematical connections

In these problems and tasks, connections are made to these other topic areas:

- arithmetic
- algebra
- graphs
- measurement
- money

Problem solving strategies

Finding Patterns and Reasoning problems and tasks offer children opportunities to use one or more of several problem solving strategies.

- **Organize Information:** To ensure that several solution candidates for a problem are considered, children may have to organize information by drawing a picture, making a list, or completing a table.

- **Guess, Check, and Revise:** In some problems, children have to identify or generate candidates for the solution and then check whether those candidates match the conditions of the problem. If the conditions are not satisfied, other possible solutions must be generated and verified.

- **Identify and Continue Patterns:** To identify the next term or terms in a sequence, children have to recognize the relationship between successive terms and then generalize that relationship.

- **Use Logic:** Children have to reason deductively, from clues, to make inferences about the solution to a problem. They have to reason inductively to continue numeric patterns.

- **Formulate Clues:** When candidates for answers are presented in displays, children must pose one or more clues for identifying one of the candidates.

- **Work Backward:** In some problems, the output is given and children must determine the input by identifying mathematical relationships between the input and output and applying inverse operations.

Communication skills

Problems and tasks in *Finding Patterns and Reasoning* are designed to stimulate communication. As part of the solution process, children may have to

- describe their thinking
- describe patterns and rules
- find alternate solution methods and solution paths
- identify other possible answers
- formulate problems for classmates to solve
- compare solutions with classmates
- make drawings to clarify mathematical relationships
- explain mathematical ideas

These communication skills are enhanced when children interact with one another and with the teacher. By communicating both orally and in writing, children develop their understanding and use of the language of mathematics.

How Can *Hot Math Topics* Be Used?

The problems may be used as practice of newly learned concepts and skills, as maintenance of previously learned ideas, and as enrichment experiences for early finishers or more advanced students.

They may be used in class or given to children to take home and do with their families. If used during class, they may be selected to complement lessons dealing with a specific topic or assigned every week as a means of keeping skills alive and well. For children whom the reading requirements of the problems exceed their current abilities, you may wish to use the problems in whole-class or group settings, where either you or an able reader presents the problems aloud.

As they become more able readers, children can work on the problems in pairs or on their own. The problems are sequenced from least to most difficult. The selection of problems may be made by the teacher or the children based on their needs or interests. If the plan is for children to choose problems, you may wish to copy individual problems onto card stock and laminate them, and establish a problem card file.

To facilitate record keeping, a Management Chart is provided on page 6. The chart can be duplicated so that there is one for each child. As a problem is completed, the space corresponding to that problem's number may be shaded. An Award Certificate is included on page 6 as well.

How Can Children's Performance Be Assessed?

Finding Patterns and Reasoning problems and tasks provide you with opportunities to assess children's

- pattern recognition and generation abilities
- mathematical reasoning methods
- knowledge of number concepts, skills, and relationships among numbers
- problem solving abilities
- communication skills

Observations

Keeping anecdotal records helps you to remember important information you gain as you observe children at work. To make observations more manageable, limit each observation to a group of from four to six children or to one of the areas noted above. You may find that using index cards facilitates the recording process.

Discussions

Many of the *Finding Patterns and Reasoning* problems and tasks allow for multiple answers or may be solved in a variety of ways. This built-in richness motivates children to discuss their work with one another. Small groups or class discussions are appropriate. As children share their approaches to the problems, you will gain additional insights into their content knowledge, mathematical reasoning, and communication abilities.

Scoring responses

You may wish to holistically score children's responses to the problems and tasks. The simple scoring rubric below uses three levels: high, medium, and low.

Portfolios

Having children store their responses to the problems in *Hot Math Topics* portfolios allows them to see improvement in their

High	Medium	Low
• Solution demonstrates that the child knows the concepts and skills.	• Solution demonstrates that the child has some knowledge of the concepts and skills.	• Solution shows that the child has little or no grasp of the concepts and skills.
• Solution is complete and thorough.	• Solution is complete.	• Solution is incomplete or contains major errors.
• The child communicates effectively.	• The child communicates somewhat clearly.	• The child does not communicate effectively.

work over time. You may want to have them choose examples of their best responses for inclusion in their permanent portfolios, accompanied by explanations as to why each was chosen.

Children and the assessment process

Involving children in the assessment process is central to the development of their abilities to reflect on their own work, to understand the assessment standards to which they are held accountable, and to take ownership for their own learning. Young children may find the reflective process difficult, but with your coaching, they can develop such skills.

Discussion may be needed to help children better understand your standards for performance. Ask children such questions as, "What does it mean to communicate *clearly*?" "What is a *complete* response?" Some children may want to use the high-medium-low rubric to score their responses. Others may prefer to use a simple visual evaluation, such as these characters:

Participation in peer-assessment tasks will also help children to better understand the performance standards. In pairs or small groups, children can review each other's responses and offer feedback. Opportunities to revise work may then be given.

What Additional Materials Are Needed?

Chips or tiles are needed in one of the tasks. Other manipulatives and materials are not required but may be helpful for some children, including unit cubes, a pan balance, a calendar, a hundred board, and sets of shapes. Colored pencils or crayons should be readily accessible. Calculators are not required for any of the tasks, although some children may find them beneficial.

Management Chart

Name _____

When a problem or task is completed, shade the box with that number.

1	2	3	4	5	6	7	8	9	10
11	12	13	14	15	16	17	18	19	20
21	22	23	24	25	26	27	28	29	30
31	32	33	34	35	36	37	38	39	40
41	42	43	44	45	46	47	48	49	50
51	52	53	54	55	56	57	58	59	60
61	62	63	64	65	66	67	68	69	70
71	72	73	74	75	76	77	78	79	80
81	82	83	84	85	86	87	88	89	90
91	92	93	94	95	96	97	98	99	100

Award Certificate

Hot Math Topics

SUPER SOLVER

this certifies that

_____

has been awarded the Hot Math Topics Super Solver Certificate for

Excellence in Problem Solving

_____   _____
date   signature

Problems
and Tasks

Row 1 ✳

Row 2 ✳ ❀

Row 3 ✳ ❀ ❀

Row 4 ✳ ❀ ❀ ❀

How many ❀ are in Row 15?
How do you know?

- -

Tell how each flag is different from the others.

Flag 1   Flag 2   Flag 3   Flag 4

Look at the shape pattern.
Draw the next two shapes.

Make up your own pattern.
Use 2 colors and 2 shapes.

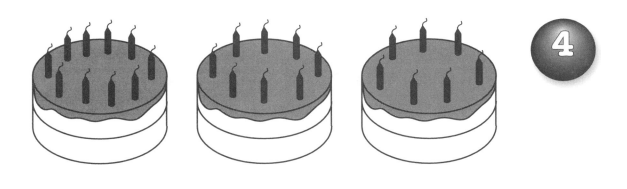

_____   _____   _____

Today is Tia, Casey, and Lila's birthday.

• Tia is older than Casey.

• Casey is older than Lila.

Write a name under each cake.

Find my number.

- It is in the circle.
- It is not in the square.
- It is greater than 1.

My number is _____.

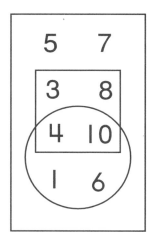

Write clues to find another number.

Have a friend find your number.

The numbers are in a pattern.

Fill in the missing numbers.

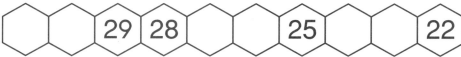

Make your own pattern with missing numbers.

Have a friend fill in the numbers.

What is the puppy's name?

- The name has the letter **a**.
- The name has fewer than 5 letters.
- The name does not begin with **S**.

The puppy's name is _____.

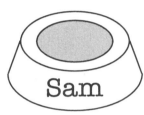 Sam

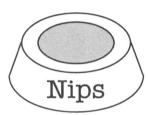 Nips

 Angel

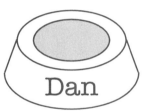 Dan

- -

Mr. Rose got on the elevator

- below the 6th floor.
- above the 3rd floor.
- not on the 5th floor.

On which floor did Mr. Rose get on the elevator?

Talk with a friend.

Tell 3 ways you are *alike*.

Tell 3 ways you are *different*.

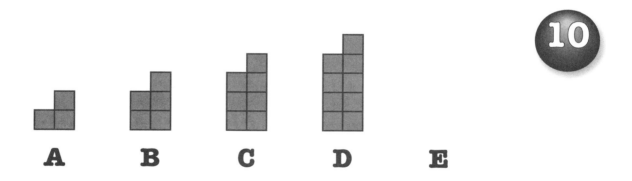

A   B   C   D   E

How many ■ do you need to make E?

Tell how you know.

Look for patterns.

Write a word that could be next.

a

be

cat

_____

Tell why your word fits the pattern.

- -

Pick a hat.

Write three clues to find the hat.

Give the clues to a friend.

Clue 1 _____

Clue 2 _____

Clue 3 _____

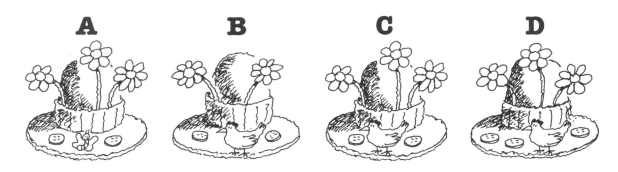

A B C D

You can show this pattern with numbers:

2, 1, 2, 1, 2, 1

Now draw a shape pattern to match these numbers:

1, 1, 2, 1, 1, 2, 1, 1, 2

Find the pattern.
Draw the missing shapes.

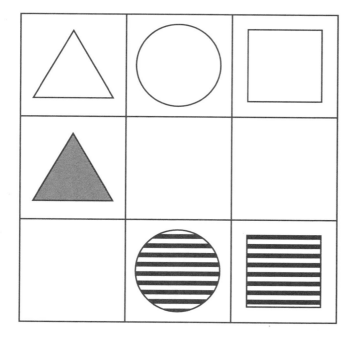

Continue the pattern.

1

  22

    333

      4444

          _____

             _____

                _____

                    _____

Keep going.
How many 9s are there?

Close your eyes.
Have a friend cover 4 of
the numbers with chips.
Open your eyes.
Tell the numbers.
Play again.

2   4   6   8   10   12   14   16

Clues

- It is less than 9 + 5.
- It is greater than 6 + 4.
- It is not 7 + 6.

My number is _____ .

How much money is in the bank?

- There is less than 40¢.
- There is more than 30¢.
- There are no pennies.

Work with a friend.

Make up a button rule.

Draw the buttons that fit the rule in the circle.

Draw the other buttons outside the circle.

Have your friend guess your rule.

19

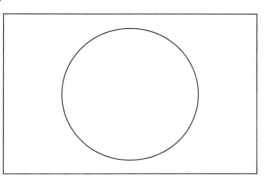

What day of the week is Jana's art class?

20

It is

- after Tuesday.
- before Friday.
- not on Wednesday

BOXBOXBOX · · ·

The pattern ends after 6 X's.

How many letters are there in all?

- -

I am an ant.
I have 6 legs.

You see 24 legs.

How many ants do you see?

Each rabbit is different.

Pick a rabbit.

Write clues.

Have a friend use the clues to find the rabbit.

23

- -

Len, Sera, Brad, and Kai found spiders.

24

• Kai found more spiders than Len.

• Brad found 2 more spiders than Sera.

• Len found 10 spiders.

Write the names in the chart.

Name	Spiders

Which robot does not belong with the others?

Tell how you decided.

Is there another answer?

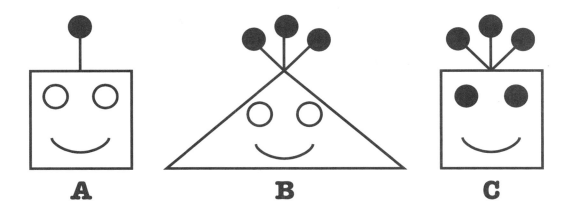

A B C

- -

Row 1

Row 2

Row 3

Row 4

How many turtles will there be in row 10?

Tell how you decided.

Row 1	1			
Row 2	2	1		
Row 3	3	2	1	
Row 4	4	3	2	1
Row 5	5	4		
Row 6				

The third number in row 4 is 2.

The third number in row 7 is _____.

Tell how you know.

- -

1	2	3	4	5	6	7	8	9	10
11	12	13	14	15	16	17	18	19	20
21	22	23	24	25	26	27	28	29	30
31	32	33	34	35	36	37	38	39	40
41	42	43	44	45	46	47	48	49	50

Color every number with a 3 in it.

What patterns do you see?

1 doll   1 ◯   2 ▫   1 ⬭   4 ▭

2 dolls   2 ◯   4 ▫   2 ⬭   8 ▭

Tell how many for 3 dolls.

___ ◯   ___ ▫   ___ ⬭   ___ ▭

- -

Fill in the circles.

1 + 3 = 4

3 + 5 = 8

5 + 7 = 12

7 + 9 = ◯

9 + ◯ = 20

Tell about 2 patterns you see.

Fill in the missing numbers.

2 ⟹ 5

3 ⟹ 6

4 ⟹ 7

5 ⟹ 8

6 ⟹ ✦

7 ⟹ ✦

8 ⟹ ✦

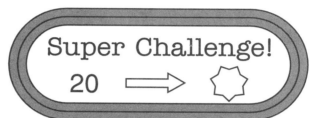

Super Challenge!

20 ⟹ ✦

How old is Pia?

• Her older sister is 15.

• Her younger brother is 12.

• Pia is not 13 years old.

Pia is _____ years old.

What comes next?

Fill in 9, 10, 11, 12, and 20.

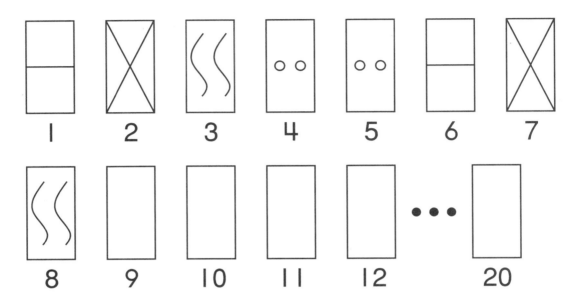

34

Who won the race?

- The winner's number is more than 20.

- The number is less than 40.

- You say the number when you count by 2s.

Row 1	✳ ✳
Row 2	✳ ✳ ✳ ✳
Row 3	✳ ✳ ✳ ✳ ✳ ✳
Row 4	✳ ✳ ✳ ✳ ✳ ✳ ✳ ✳
Row 5	✳ ✳ ✳ ✳ ✳ ✳

How many ✳ are in row 6?

Tell how you know.

- -

Today is Tuesday.

I play ball 3 days after tomorrow.

On which day do I play ball?

Match each stick to a dog.

- Sal's stick is the shortest.
- Meg's stick is shorter than Fido's.
- Joe's stick is the longest.

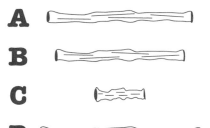

A
B
C
D

Fido   Sal   Joe   Meg

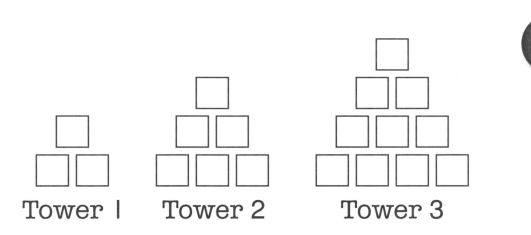

Tower 1   Tower 2   Tower 3

Draw tower 5.

How many ☐ did you draw?

Pick two numbers from those shown. Add.

How many different sums can you make? Make a list.

- -

 **+**  **= 12¢**

 **+** = **15¢**

 **= _____ ¢**  **= _____ ¢**

 The **weighs 8 pounds.**

What could the  **weigh?**
Tell how you know.

- -

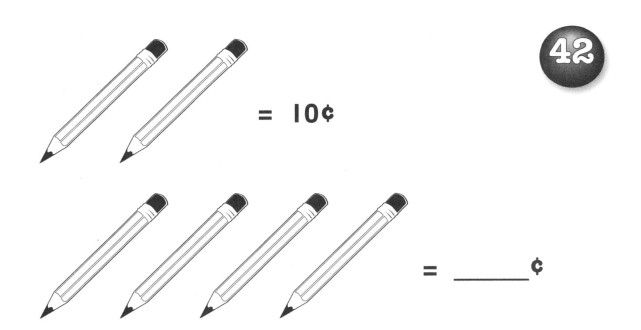

= 10¢

= _____ ¢

Tell how you know.

You have 4 boxes of toys like this one.

Altogether, how many

- do you have?

- do you have?

- do you have?

Find the number pattern.

Write numbers in the blank .

Kristi is standing in line.

I am second in line. Four children are behind me.

How many children are behind the first person in line?

- -

Put an X on the shape that fits the facts.

Facts

- It has corners.
- It has more than 3 sides.
- All the sides are not the same length.

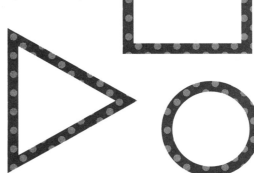

Tell two ways to get the answer.

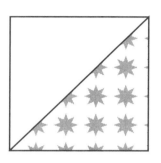 = 18

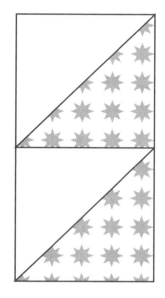 = _____

Draw the parade.

- The bird is first in the parade.
- The dog is last.
- The cat is after the snake.
- The rabbit is right in front of the dog.

Write the ages.

I am 3 + 3 years old.

I am twice as old as Mara.

I am 2 years younger than Tina.

Tina

Nigel

Mara

_____ **years old**   _____ **years old**   _____ **years old**

- -

How many bones are in your hand?

Find the correct number from the sign.

- There are more than 10.
- You say the number when you count by 3s.
- The number of bones is not 9 + 9.

7	27
22	18

You and a friend are toasting marshmallows.

- You eat 4 marshmallows.
- Your friend eats 4 marshmallows.
- There are 5 marshmallows left.

How many marshmallows did you have at the start?

51

All of these are flibbles.

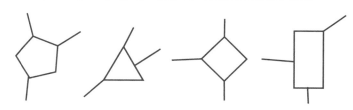

52

None of these are flibbles.

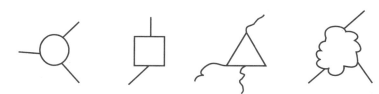

Which of these is a flibble? Why?

    A   **B**   **C**   **D**

Suppose you write the numbers 1, 2, 3, 4, . . ., through 50.

Will you write more 1s or more 9s?

How did you decide?

Add.

Look for patterns.

8	18	28	38		☆
+ 2	+ 2	+ 2	+ 2	. . .	+ 2
					80

Fill in the ☆ **.**

Write the names of the friends from tallest to shortest.

_____ _____ _____ _____

tallest   shortest

José — I am taller than Kara.

Eric — I am shorter than Kara.

Ana — I am the shortest.

Kara — I am taller than Ana.

The pattern continues.

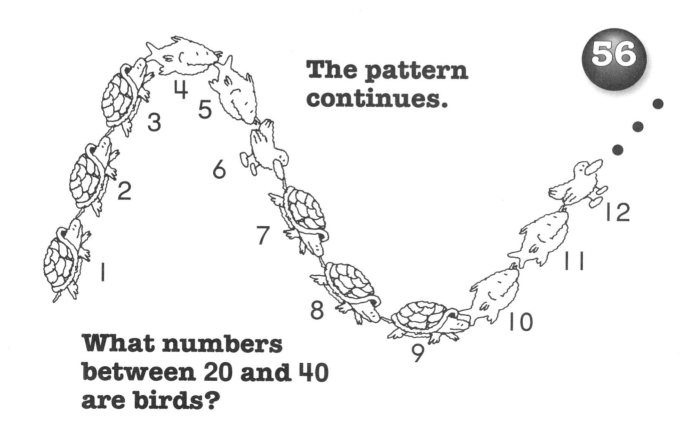

What numbers between 20 and 40 are birds?

Use the numbers 1, 1, 1, 1, 10, and 10.

Put one number in each circle.

The three numbers in each line must add to 12.

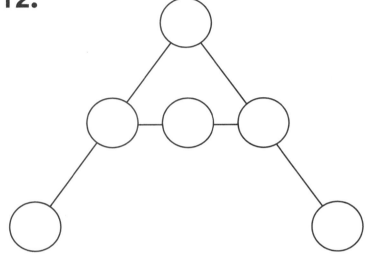

- -

I have two coins. **58**

Together they are

- less than 25¢.

- more than 2¢.

What coins could I have?

How many stars are on a U.S. flag?

The number is on the bird's flag.

- The number of stars is between 30 and 70.
- The number in the tens place is greater than 4.
- The number in the ones place is less than 1.

Draw 2 bracelets like this.

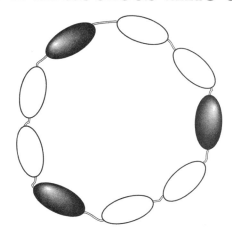

How many of each did you draw?

◯ = _____   ⬭ = _____

In 5 bracelets, how many would you draw?

◯ = _____   ⬭ = _____

Picture A   **Picture B**   **Picture C**

1 △   2 △   3 △

3 ○   6 ○   9 ○

Another picture has 6 △.
How many ○ does it have?

- -

Who has the most books?
How do you know?

I have 5 fewer books then Beth.

I have twice as many as Alex.

I have 11 books.

The sum of three numbers is 18.

- One number is 8.
- One number is more than 8.

What could the third number be?

Which fence is longer:

the rectangle fence   **or**   the square fence

Tell how you know.

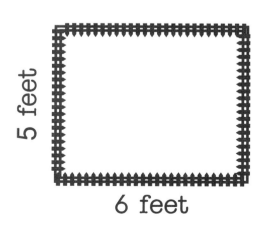

5 feet

6 feet

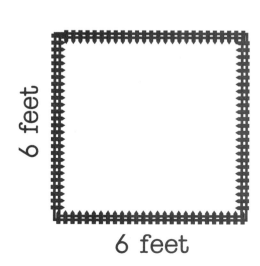

6 feet

6 feet

© Dale Seymour Publications®

Two frogs start jumping at 1.

- The 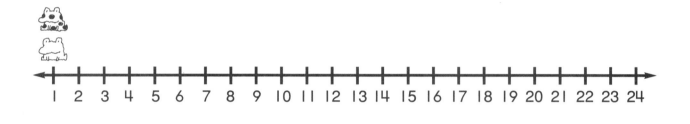 jumps in a +2 pattern.

- The jumps in a +3 pattern.

Write the numbers where both frogs will land.

1 2 3 4 5 6 7 8 9 10 11 12 13 14 15 16 17 18 19 20 21 22 23 24

1	2	3	4	5	6	7	8	9	10
11	12	13	14	15	16	17	18	19	20
21	22	23	24	25	26	27	28	29	30
31	32	33	34	35	36	37	38	39	40
41	42	43	44	45	46	47	48	49	50

Color the numbers you say when you count by 3s.

What patterns do you see?

Draw stickers to fit the facts.

- Ang has 12 stickers.
- He has ♡, ☺, and ☾ stickers.
- He has fewer ♡ than ☺ stickers.
- He has fewer ☾ than ♡ stickers.
- He has 6 ☺ stickers.

How many different answers can you find?

Write the start number.

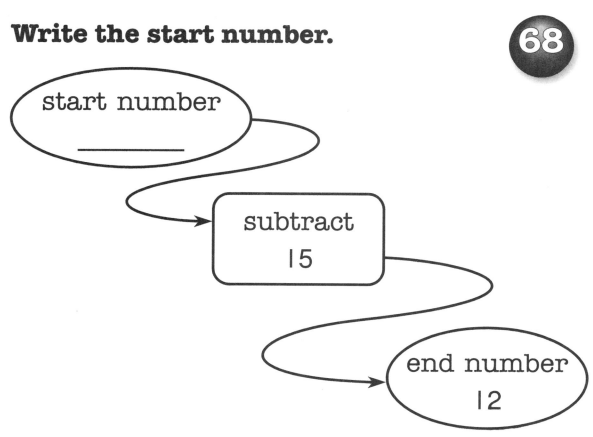

start number

_____

subtract 15

end number 12

The number pattern continues.

2	6	10	14	18	22
4	8	12	16	20	24

Follow the arrows.

Fill in the missing numbers.

$8 \rightarrow = 12$ $16 \leftarrow \leftarrow = 8$ $4 \rightarrow \rightarrow \leftarrow = 8$

$18 \rightarrow = \underline{\quad}$ $14 \rightarrow \rightarrow = \underline{\quad}$ $22 \leftarrow = \underline{\quad}$

$6 \rightarrow \rightarrow \leftarrow = \underline{\quad}$ $22 \rightarrow = \underline{\quad}$ $30 \rightarrow \rightarrow = \underline{\quad}$

- -

Continue the doubles pattern.

$1 + 3 = 2 + 2$

$1 + 5 = 3 + 3$

$1 + 7 = 4 + 4$

$1 + 9 = \bigcirc + \bigcirc$

$1 + 11 = \bigcirc + \bigcirc$

$1 + 13 = \bigcirc + \bigcirc$

$1 + 15 = \bigcirc + \bigcirc$

> **Super Challenge!**
>
> $1 + 99 = \bigcirc + \bigcirc$

How many keys are on a piano?

71

Clues

- The number is greater than 30 + 33.
- The number is less than 100.
- The ones digit is between 3 and 9.

62 93 88 79 104

Make a rule.

72

- Use your rule to put these shapes into 2 groups.
- Tell your rule.
- Draw the shapes in each group.

Make another rule.

Put the shapes into new groups.

Row 1 | 1 | 2 | 3 | 4 | 5 |
Row 2 | 6 | 7 | 8 | 9 | 10 |
Row 3 | 11 | 12 | 13 | 14 | 15 |
Row 4 | 16 | 17 | 18 | 19 | 20 |
Row 5 | 21 | 22 | 23 | 24 | 25 |

5 is at the end of row 1.

What is at the end of

row 6? _____   row 7? _____   row 10? _____

Which is heavier,  **or**  **?**
How can you tell?

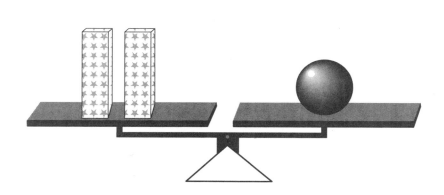

© Dale Seymour Publications®

4 wheels   8 wheels   12 wheels

How many wheels do 10 cars have?

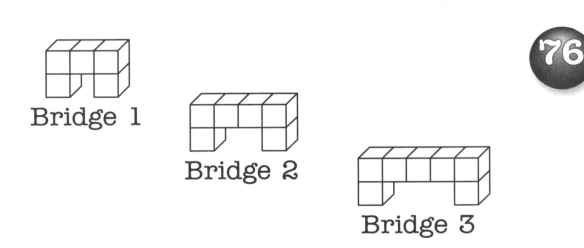

Bridge 1

Bridge 2

Bridge 3

Bridge 10 has more ▢ than bridge 2.

How many more?

The letter pattern continues.

In the first 12 letters,
how many letters are

- P? _____
- U? _____
- R? _____

In the first 24 letters,
how many letters are

- P? _____
- U? _____
- R? _____

- -

Find the pattern.

Draw the missing tiles.

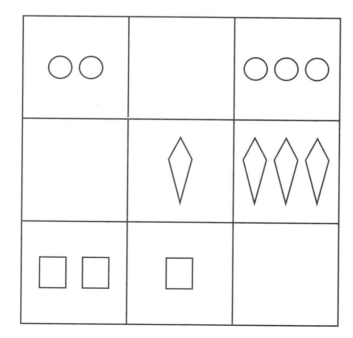

Eight numbers are sorted into 2 groups.

Tell how you think the numbers are sorted.

Write a new number in each square.

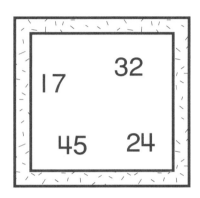

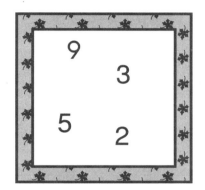

All of these are morks.

None of these are morks.

Which of these are morks? Why?

A **B** **C** **D**

Draw cookies on the plates to fit the facts.

- There are 10 cookies.
- There are more cookies on plate A than on plate B.
- There are more cookies on plate C than on plate A.

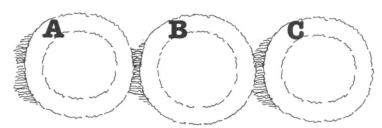

Compare your answers with a friend.

- -

Shikara makes bracelets like this.

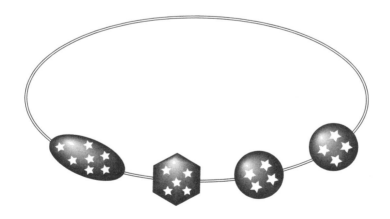

She has 20 ⬭, 20 ⬡, and 20 ●.
How many bracelets can she make?

Put numbers in the shapes.

Put the same numbers in the same shapes.

⬡ + ⬡ = 8

⬡ + ☆ = 13

⬡ = _____   ☆ = _____

Who has the fewest marbles?

I have 3 more marbles than Peter.

I have half as many marbles as Carlos.

I have 2 more marbles than Taylor.

Taylor   **Peter**   **Carlos**

If A = 10, then B = _____ .

- -

How old are Meg and Sam?

- Their ages add to 9.
- Meg is 1 year older than Sam.

Meg is ____ years old.

Sam is ____ years old.

Meg   Sam

Fill in the squares.

87

- Add across.
- Add down.

The numbers in the circles are sums.

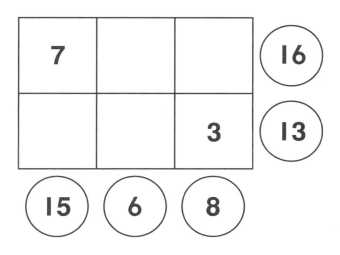

Write the start number.

88

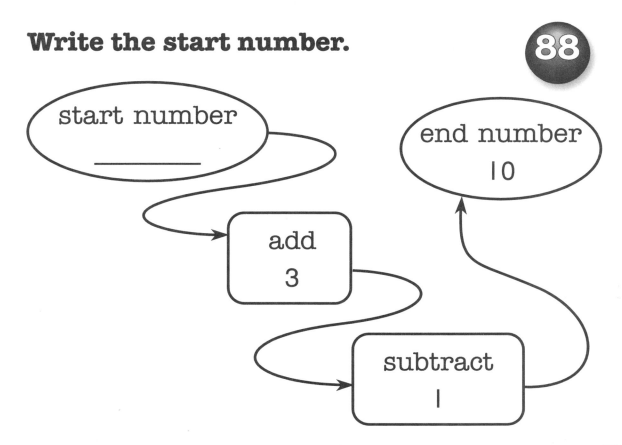

The number pattern continues.

1	3	5	7	9	11
2	4	6	8	10	12

Follow the arrows.
Fill in the missing numbers.

$7 \rightarrow = 9$ $10 \leftarrow \leftarrow = 6$ $4 \rightarrow \rightarrow = 8$

$8 \rightarrow = \underline{\quad}$ $7 \rightarrow \rightarrow = \underline{\quad}$ $11 \leftarrow = \underline{\quad}$

$6 \rightarrow \rightarrow \leftarrow = \underline{\quad}$ $17 \rightarrow = \underline{\quad}$ $20 \leftarrow \leftarrow = \underline{\quad}$

- -

Sticker Swap

Trade  for  .

How many for  ?

Draw the next 4 shapes.

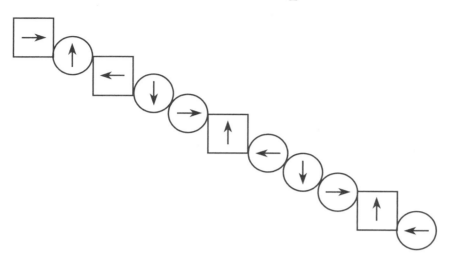

___

___

___

___

- -

The scales balance.

Make up weights for each block.

= ____ pounds   = ____ pounds

= ____ pounds

Compare your answers with a friend.

How many different answers can you find?

The pattern continues.

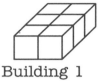
Building 1

Building 2

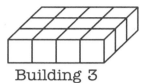
Building 3

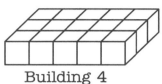
Building 4

How many are in

- building 5? _____
- building 6? _____
- building 10? _____
- building 20? _____

- -

Fill in the empty squares and circle.

- Add across.
- Add down.

The numbers in the circles are sums.

3			⑫
	5		⑪
⑦	◯	③	

Think of a hundred board.
Fill in the missing numbers.

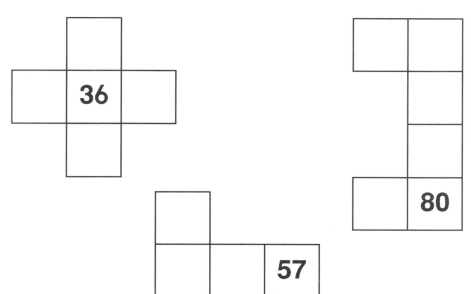

The number pattern continues.

1	4	7	10	13	16
2	5	8	11	14	17
3	6	9	12	15	18

Follow the arrows.
Fill in the missing numbers.

$7 \rightarrow = 10$ $10 \leftarrow \leftarrow = 4$ $6 \rightarrow \rightarrow = 12$

$15 \rightarrow = \underline{\hphantom{00}}$ $7 \rightarrow \rightarrow = \underline{\hphantom{00}}$ $11 \leftarrow = \underline{\hphantom{00}}$

$14 \rightarrow \rightarrow = \underline{\hphantom{00}}$ $10 \rightarrow \rightarrow \leftarrow = \underline{\hphantom{00}}$ $20 \leftarrow \leftarrow = \underline{\hphantom{00}}$

What's the mystery number?

- It is between 0 and 49.
- You say it when you count by 5s.
- You don't say it when you count by 10s.
- The tens digit is between 1 and 3.

The number is _____ .

- -

Which kite is Shondra's?

- Half of it is striped.
- It has 4 bows.

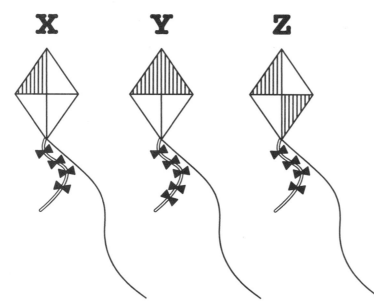

X   Y   Z

How many different ways can you put these boxes in a row?

Make drawings of fruits to show the ways.

99

Tell what's funny about what **says.**

100

I have 1 quart of water.

I have more water than you do. I have 4 cups. And 4 is more than 1.

Answers

1. 14; It is 1 less than the row number.

2. Possible answer: flag 1: only 1 circle; flag 2: only 1 square; flag 3: only 4 stars; flag 4: 4 stripes

3. ○○; Patterns will vary.

4. Tia, Casey, Lila

5. 6; Clues will vary.

6. 31, 30, 27, 26, 24, 23; Patterns will vary.

7. Dan

8. 4th floor

10. 11; Explanations will vary.

11. Possible answer: Door; it begins with *d* and has 4 letters.

12. Clues will vary.

13. Patterns will vary.

14.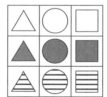

15. 55555, 666666, 7777777, 88888888; 9 nines

17. 12

18. 35¢

19. Rules will vary.

20. Thursday

21. 18 letters

22. 4 ants

23. Clues will vary.

24. Kai, Sera, Brad, Len

25. Possible answers: A; it has 1 antenna and the others have 3. B; it has a triangular face and the others are square. C; it has black eyes and the others have white eyes.

26. 11; It is 1 more than the row number.

27. 5; Explanations will vary.

28. All the numbers are in the same row or column, except for 30.

29. 3, 6, 3, 12

30. $7 + 9 = 16, 9 + 11 = 20$; Possible patterns: The sums differ by 4; two odd numbers are added; the sum is twice the even number between the odd numbers.

31. 9, 10, 11, 23

32. 14

33.

9 10 11 12 ... 20

34. 26

35. 12; Possible explanation: The number of ✳ increases by 2 for each row, so row 5 has 10 ✳ and row 6 has 12 ✳.

36. Saturday

37. Fido, A; Meg, B; Sal, C; Joe, D

38. 21

39. 5 sums: $2 + 3 = 5, 2 + 4 = 6, 2 + 5 = 7$ (and $3 + 4 = 7$), $3 + 5 = 8, 4 + 5 = 9$

40. 7¢, 8¢

41. Anything less than 8 pounds. Explanations will vary.

42. 20¢; Possible explanations: 4 is twice 2, and twice 10¢ is 20¢. *Or,* 2 pencils for 10¢ is 1 pencil for 5¢ and 4 pencils for 4 × 5¢ = 20¢.

43. 12 balls, 8 cars, 4 dolls

44. 40, 25

45. 5 children

46. rectangle

47. 36; Possible explanations: is two ◿ so the value is twice 18, or 36. *Or,* each triangle is 9 and there are four triangles in ◿, and 4 × 9 = 36.

48. from first to last: bird, snake, cat, rabbit, dog

49. 6, 8, 4

50. 27

51. 13 marshmallows

52. A; Possible explanation: A flibble is a polygon with three straight lines sticking out of it.

53. more 1s; Explanations will vary.

54. 10, 20, 30, 40, 78

55. José, Kara, Eric, Ana

56. 24, 30, 36

57.

58. penny and nickel, penny and dime, 2 nickels, nickel and dime, 2 dimes

59. 50 stars

60. 12, 6; 30, 15

61. 18

62. Tanya; Possible explanation: Beth has 11 books, Alex has 6 books, and Tanya has 12 books.

63. Possible answers: 1 (if the second number is 9) or 0 (if the second number is 10)

64. the square fence; Possible explanation: The square fence is 6 + 6 + 6 + 6 = 24 feet; the rectangle fence is 6 + 5 + 6 + 5 = 22 feet.

65. 7, 13, 19

66. Possible answer: There are 2 numbers between each colored number. The colored numbers form diagonal lines.

67.

♡	☺	☾
5	6	1
4	6	2

68. 27

69. 22, 22, 18, 10, 26, 38

70. 1 + 9 = 5 + 5, 1 + 11 = 6 + 6, 1 + 13 = 7 + 7, 1 + 15 = 8 + 8, 1 + 99 = 50 + 50

71. 88

72. Rules will vary.

73. 30, 35, 50

74. the sphere; Possible explanation: Each block is half the weight of a sphere.

75. 40 wheels

76. 8

77. 3, 3, 6; 6, 6, 12

78.

79. Possible answer: They are sorted by whether they have 1 or 2 digits. New numbers will vary.

80. A and D; Possible explanation: A mork has 4 sides surrounding a star and a triangle.

81. Possible answers:

A	B	C
4	1	5
3	2	5
3	1	6

82. 10 bracelets

83. 4, 9

84. Peter

85. 30

86. 5, 4

87.

7	4	5	(16)
8	2	3	(13)
(15)	(6)	(8)	

88. 8

89. 10, 11, 9, 8, 19, 16

90. 6

91.

92. There is an infinite number of answers. Any answer in which the 🁢 is half the weight of the 🌐, and in which the 🌐 weighs the same as the ⬡, is correct.

93. 18, 21, 33, 63

94.

3	8	1	(12)
4	5	2	(11)
(7)	(13)	(3)	

95.

	26			49	50
35	36	37			60
	46				70
				79	80

	45	
55	56	57

96. 18, 13, 8, 20, 13, 14

97. 25

98. Z

99. 6 ways: grape, orange, apple; grape, apple, orange; orange, apple, grape; orange, grape, apple; apple, orange, grape; apple, grape, orange

100. They have the same amount of water: 4 cups equals 1 quart.